Chopping Wood
and
Carrying Water
…One Day at a Time

**Break out of Destructive Patterns and Realize
Your Potential**

**A 30 day Devotional based on the Recovering
way of life**

Paul J. Wolanin MA, CADC

Chop Wood and Carry Water. Repeat.

*"I can do all things through Christ who
strengthens me."*
- Philippian 4:13

Paul J. Wolanin

http://freedomthroughchange.com

Ordering Information:

Quantity sales. Special discounts are available on quantity purchases by corporations, associations, and others. For details, contact the "Special Sales Department" at the address above.

Chopping Wood and Carrying Water

Paul J. Wolanin -- 1st ed.

ISBN 978-1493710898

This book is dedicated to my beautiful wife for putting up with a lot of very early mornings. Living with me must be a feat in itself! Thank you for your unconditional love and support…

For my Mom: you are my inspiration!

For my brothers:
Ride to Live & Live to Ride

<u>Serenity Prayer</u>

God grant me the serenity
To accept the things I cannot change;
Courage to change the things I can;
And wisdom to know the difference.
Living one day at a time;
Enjoying one moment at a time;
Accepting hardships as the pathway to
peace;
Taking, as He did, this sinful world as it
is,
Not as I would have it;
Trusting that He will make all things
right if I surrender to His Will;
That I may be reasonably happy in this
life
And supremely happy with Him forever
in the next.
Amen.

Reinhold Niebuhr

Before reading this little devotional, please consider one thing:

Those who cannot change their minds cannot change anything.

— George Bernard Shaw

Introduction

I am just like any other guy trying to figure out this journey we call life. If there is one thing that I have learned so far, it is that life rarely makes complete sense. Life is rarely fair, and life is about as hard as I make it out to be. For most of my time on earth, I lived my life as if *nothing* were possible. I lived as a victim of circumstance. I took things as they came and just figured that some people were meant to make it and some people were not. I had subscribed to the belief for a long time that I was one of those unfortunates who was just not meant to live within the boundaries of normal society. I was one of those people that for whatever reason was meant to live life on the edge: a life filled with jails, institutions, drugs, alcohol and *complete insanity*. A life without any real hope for the future, a life in which I doubted I would ever see my thirtieth birthday. Living a life in active addiction is hell on earth. If you have been there, I need not explain myself further. If you have *not* been there, be glad.

Many years ago, God presented me with a choice which was clear as day: **CHANGE OR DIE.** I had seen the worst parts of myself and the worst parts of humanity. I was living my life in a manner which could be likened to playing Russian roulette with *all* the bullets; there were dozens and dozens of times that I should have been killed, should have died, or should have been locked away *forever* but was not. It occurred to me one day that my "luck" – as I used to believe – was certainly running out. One day, lying sick as a dog in a detox center outside of Detroit, I started to think of God. I wondered if *He* was the One who kept stopping those proverbial bullets from taking my life. He must have been. I could not find any other explanation. All of the times I had narrowly escaped death, all of the times I should not have woken up after some very hard nights of mixing whiskey and cocaine, all the times I should have been shot and killed, and the times I could have killed someone else. I was still here. I was in pretty rough shape physically, mentally, emotionally - and completely broken spiritually - but I was still here. *God must have a plan for me,* I began to tell myself that day in detox, with the stench of stale cigarette smoke on my clothes and whiskey leaching out of my pours. ***God must have a plan for me. He just has to. I should be dead.***

I choose to share what my life *was* like in order to share with you what my life is like *now.* As I mentioned, I used to live my life as a victim of circumstance. I used to live my life as if *nothing* were possible. Today, I live my life with hope, knowing that *anything* is possible with sobriety and an unshakable faith in the One who *saved my ass*, time and time again. I choose to call that One God. You might be thinking *"Wow, good for you, Paul. Way to go, buddy. But what does this have to do with me?"* Well, *my* story is probably not unlike *your* story. Just how is that so? Maybe you have never used drugs, been arrested or jailed or never drank yourself to the point of oblivion. That is okay. Having lived a life of active addiction is not a requirement to have something in common with me. I can almost guarantee that you are struggling with some part of your life; that is where our similarities convene.

Most people seem to deal with the same self-defeating behaviors: depression, anxiety, worry, procrastination, negative thinking and FEAR of the future. If *any* part of your life is not to your liking this book is for *you.* Whether you are a recovering person, a person *thinking* about getting into recovery, a working professional with a six-figure salary, a stay at home mom, a student, grandparent, or just about anyone else - this book was written just for you.

I am certainly not an all-out expert on the subjects of addiction, recovery, or self-improvement, but I would like to think that I know enough to write this book. In the past thirty-something years, I have seen the gates of hell with my own two eyes. I have sat and had a drink and a smoke with Satan himself. I was working for the fallen angel, doing his bidding and not caring who got hurt. Thanks to God, I managed to live to talk about it. I have learned a lot of things along the way from those that came before me. What I've found, above all else, is that recovery is *work*. Recovery is *hard work*. Life in general is hard work – at least if you want to live a good one. This book will be difficult for you to read. It is meant to be. *Most of us,*

recovering or not, lead lives of quiet desperation.
Lives that are dictated by the status quo. Lives that
could be better. However, most people do not
know how to go about making the necessary
changes to actually *make life better*. So just what
can be done to get your life where you want it to
be? The answer is in the title of this book: by
**CHOPPING WOOD AND CARRYING
WATER.**

What the title of this book refers to is hard work -
done day in and day out. It actually comes from a
Zen proverb: *"Before enlightenment, chop wood
and carry water; after enlightenment, chop wood
and carry water."* It speaks to not only hard work
and repetition, but to staying in the moment and
focusing on the task at hand. Chopping wood and
carrying water are things that we may not *want* to
do every day, but things that will give us a solid
foundation in our lives and in our recovery.
Chopping wood and carrying water is hard work,
but work worth doing. Give this book a try. If you
don't like how your life is going after a month,
your misery will gladly be refunded.

<u>Day 1</u>

"Whether you think you can, or think you can't, you are right."
- Henry Ford

The human mind is a powerful thing. It has the power to create and the power to destroy. It can lead us to a place of happiness and serenity - or lead us to a place of depression, desperation and fear. What we think determines who we are and what we do. What is the difference between a person of great confidence and a person paralyzed by insecurity and fear? What is the difference between someone who lives a life free of limitations, judgments and self-imposed boundaries; and someone who is living life as a prisoner of their own mind? It may seem all too simple of an answer. The difference between these types of people is the ***manner in which they think.*** It is the flavor, the color and the content of what they choose to think about at any given moment that determines the quality of their lives. Are you with me on this? It is surely an easy concept, but one that is incredibly difficult to apply. As the title of this little book suggests, changing the way you think can be likened to chopping wood and carrying water: something that is hard work and something that *must* be done daily. But you *can* do it, as long as you give it a fair trial.

For the majority of my life prior to entering recovery I was told that I would probably never amount to anything. I heard this from teachers, coaches, employers and probation officers. Granted, I was living the kind of life that was nothing to be proud of: dope, booze, crime and layer upon layer of lies. Even before I began using substances as my "answer" to life's problems I knew had a *thinking problem*. I felt that my best was never good enough and that I didn't quite measure up to others. I felt that other kids were always better than me in some way – smarter, more handsome, better on the football field, more popular and so on. I was the angry kid that didn't get along with anyone.

All the messages I heard growing up began to take root in my mind. "You are going to end up in prison!" or "You are just not smart enough to graduate, you're going to have to attend summer school just to catch up!*"* or my personal favorite was something my pee-wee football coach used to tell me "Son, some people are just not cut out to be winners in life!*"* That one really burned. I played it off as Mr. Cool, that *I don't give a rip what others think of me*, but inside I was torn apart. Years and years of these types of messages became tattooed in my mind and these messages became the basis for all my thoughts from that point forward. Remember this: ***we are all products of the messages we have heard throughout our lives, whether the messages are true or not.*** Just because someone tells you that you can't do something, can't be something, or can't achieve something *means nothing*. This is their opinion of you and nothing else. We never know what truly motivates a person to say the things that they do. They are probably hurting too. *If you are living your life believing that you have limitations, living your life based on messages you have heard from others, you are not living to your true potential.* Your thinking is wrong and has probably been wrong for some time. The good news is that you can start right now, *today*, to transform the way you think. And this is how.

As the Apostle Paul has written in **Romans 12:2, "And be not conformed to this world: but be transformed by the renewing of your mind, that you may prove what is the good, and acceptable, and perfect, will of God."** *Be transformed by the renewing of your mind.* This passage does not say that our lives will change a little; it states that we will be *transformed*. To be *transformed* means that we will make a thorough and dramatic change in the form, appearance, or character of our lives. That is a pretty hefty promise, to say the least, but it is true.

In order to being transforming your mind, here is what you need to do: For the next 24 hours, I want you to write down *for every hour you are awake* what you are thinking about. That's right - *every hour* I want you to write down what messages you have been telling yourself (we are always talking to ourselves.) You don't need to concern yourself with recording things like "I was thinking about the Lion's game" or "I was thinking about what I need to get at the grocery store." What you need to focus on are ***themes of thought.*** A theme of thought is essentially the negative or positive *label* you assign to your thoughts. So for example, from 7 am. until 8 am. your entry might be "I've been thinking about where my mortgage payment is going to come from…how I am so lonely, depressed, or scared…what my coworkers think about me…what might happen at tomorrow's meeting…how I'm too fat/skinny/short/tall," and so on. Keep this journal for the next 24 hours. Do not look at what you have written until you read tomorrow's devotional.

Day 2

"Garbage in, garbage out!" - Unknown

I love to ride my motorcycle. I pack up and get out of town as often as I can. I love the wind in my face, the bugs in my teeth and the smells, sights and sounds you can only experience on two wheels. Part of being on the road is eating out excessively. A greasy sausage biscuit for breakfast, untold numbers of energy drinks and protein bars, hamburgers and French fries for lunch and maybe a pizza for dinner. Granted, I could eat a much healthier diet on the road if I chose to, but part of the fun of being in the wind is hitting all the little restaurants along the way.

After a few days of eating a fast-food diet, I tend to feel bloated, lethargic, and generally unhealthy. I get heartburn, I am tired and I feel weak. I am feeling bad physically because of the food I have been putting into my body – eat like crap, feel like crap. That is about as simple as it gets. Once I am home from a trip, I immediately get back to my normal diet. I eat fairly healthy – lots of chicken, beef, vegetables and good carbohydrates. I like to exercise and as my good friend always reminds me, *"Muscle is made in the kitchen, not the gym!"* After a few days of eating right, my body begins to feel normal again. My energy levels come back, I am able to concentrate more and I even sleep better. I start to feel better *mentally* just because I'm eating better. **Eat well, feel well.** Again, a simple concept.

Take out your thought log from yesterday and place it in front of you. Imagine that your thoughts are food. Take a careful look at your *thought diet* – what did you feed yourself yesterday? Did you have resentment for breakfast, worry for lunch and self-condemnation for dinner? What did you snack on between meals? Guilt? Shame? Remorse? Take a very careful look at what your thought diet consisted of these last 24 hours. If you are wondering why you have been feeling defeated, depressed, worried and hopeless, just take a look at what you've been feeding your brain! *Garbage in, garbage out.* **What we habitually think about eventually manifests in our lives.**

Referring to your thought log, take a highlighter and mark every self-defeating, negative, or worrisome thought from yesterday. Now create an alternate thought to replace the negative thought. For example: if you have highlighted "I am stuck in a dead end job" or "I never have enough money" or "I am never going to find that special someone to spend my life with" I want you to *completely change the theme of your thinking*, and this is how.

Replace every negative, self-defeating and limiting thought with a thought that is positive and true. If you have highlighted "I am never going to find that special someone to spend my life with," it is no use to think "I am going to find that special someone today" if you are not prepared to take certain steps. You might consider thinking "Today is the day that I am going to talk to that certain someone at the office, at the coffee shop, or in line at the grocery store; I am going to start with saying hello and take it from there." If you highlighted "I am working a dead end job," you might replace that thought with "Today I will apply to a job that will be more fulfilling, or research college courses to further my job opportunities." These types of thoughts take you from being a *victim* to taking *control* over the areas of your life which you can.

The crux of these exercises is that *you must be willing to take action on these thoughts.* On a 3x5 index card, write down the thoughts you want to think today (yes, you *can* choose what you think about - even if you are still having doubts, do it anyway.) Keep the card somewhere you can reference it throughout the day (I keep mine in my wallet.) Refer to this index card a minimum of 10, 20, 30 or 40 times a day and remember: *What you feed your mentality you will begin to experience in your reality.* This may not happen overnight, but nothing worth doing ever does. Keep this practice up for the rest of the day and I can guarantee you will begin to see life like you have never seen it before. After a week of changing the thought-food you are feeding your mentality, you will feel better. After a few weeks, this manner of thinking will become a *habit*. You will begin to know a new freedom, your reality will change and you will begin to know a way of life that you once thought impossible. Keep chopping wood and carrying water. Do the work of changing your thoughts. Just for today.

Day 3

"There are two primary choices in life: to accept conditions as they exist, or accept the responsibility for changing them"
– Dennis Waitley

How much time do you spend worrying? Have you ever thought about this? If you have made your thought list and examined it, I bet you have found that you spend *a lot* of time worrying about things. If you are anything like most people, you likely worry about the future: financial issues, occupational issues, relationships, your health, dying and why you are not further ahead in life. You also probably think a lot about the past: missed opportunities, mistakes, resentments and things you have done and said. Have you really ever considered just how much time you spend thinking about things in your life that are out of your control? Would you like to have a healthier outlook on life and continue to move from the **victim** role into a role of **empowerment** and **self-fulfillment?** Have you ever considered making a list? I know, I know…another list? The list I am going to ask you to make next will tie directly into the work you have done the last few days.

This list will be based loosely on the Serenity Prayer common in 12-step groups:

"God, grant me the serenity; to accept the things I cannot change; Courage to change the things I

can; and wisdom to know the difference."
-Reinhold Niebuhr

For the purpose of today's exercise in change, we are going to focus on the second and third lines of this awesome little prayer (and this is only the short form.) On a fresh sheet of paper in your journal, write down THINGS I CAN CHANGE and at the top of the page. On another sheet in your journal, write THINGS I CANNOT CHANGE. I want you to really spend some time on this list. Think carefully about the things you can and cannot change; be as detailed as possible and do not forget to pray for Devine inspiration. This is an all-inclusive list and should contain every single aspect of your life. Do not hold back. Do not rush and do not skimp. Most importantly, be *honest* about the things you can and cannot change. *Honesty* is the *key* to this exercise and remember this: We cannot change other people. We cannot change how they think, how they behave, or the actions they take. **We can only change ourselves.**

Most of us spend countless hours every single day thinking things such as "If only he/she would see things my way…if only my boss treated me better…if only I had been born into a different family…if only my kids would behave…if only I lived somewhere else…if only I had my own home…if only I had a newer car" and so on. This type of thinking drains us of energy, is highly unproductive and represents a victim attitude. But all this *can* change, if you are sincerely willing to do the work. Carefully review your list. Go about the business of enjoying your day and know that you are on the path. You have just begun.

Day 4

"And acceptance is the answer to all my problems today."
-The Big Book of Alcoholics Anonymous, 4th ed.

Have you ever given any real thought to the above statement? As the Big Book of Alcoholics Anonymous tells us, acceptance is the answer to *all* of our problems today. Not some of our problems - not just our drinking or drug problems, our problems with food, sex, gambling, or the internet, but *all* of our problems. Do you not think this is true? Think about this: are you where you want to be in your life at this moment? Are you living the kind of life you really want to be living? Are your relationships exactly how you want them to be? Do you like your job? How are your finances? What about your health? Do you need to lose a few pounds, quit smoking, or start exercising?

My guess is that you are not exactly where you want to be in life and this is why: *You are fighting.* You are fighting the fact that you dislike your job. You are angry at your spouse, parents, friends, or co-workers. You are broke, or you do not feel that you are earning enough money to meet your financial obligations. Maybe you have gotten a little thick around the middle in the last year. It is not your current reality which needs to change, but your level of acceptance.

As the Big Book of Alcoholics Anonymous says, *"When I am disturbed, it is because I find some person, place, thing, or situation – some fact of my life – unacceptable to me, and I can find no serenity until I accept that person, place, thing, or situation as being exactly the way it is supposed to be at this moment."*

Referring to your lists of THINGS I CAN CHANGE and THINGS I CANNOT CHANGE, take a close look at the areas of your life you are truly powerless to do anything about, THE THINGS I CANNOT CHANGE. Part of your unhappiness, depression, discouragement and hopelessness is that you have been focusing your energy on things you cannot do anything about. THE THINGS YOU CANNOT CHANGE YOU MUST LEARN TO ACCEPT.

Accepting the things you cannot change does not mean you have to agree with these things. It does not mean you have to like these things or believe that these things are fair. The goal is to move towards an *attitude of acceptance* - that is the crux of the whole idea behind this exercise, the key to happiness and serenity and a stepping stone to a new way of life.

Refer to your list of THINGS I CANNOT CHANGE again. Each morning, afternoon, or evening – better yet, all throughout the day – begin to pray for acceptance of these things. Ask God or your Higher Power to help you. If you are not quite there yet, ask your Higher Power for the *willingness* to accept these things. And remember, attempting to pray is praying. Expect immediate results if you are sincerely asking for help with acceptance. Keep this practice up for the rest of the day, tomorrow and whenever you begin to struggle with acceptance of the things you cannot change. Get ready and roll up your sleeves, because the real work of changing your life begins on the next page.

Day 5

"Through change comes freedom"- Unknown

The last few days we have spent time changing the way we think. In order to produce any long lasting change in our mentality, it is important to keep our thoughts productive and positive. Remember, what you feed your brain is the *thought-food* that determines how you will feel and what actions you will take. Spare no expense to constantly monitor your habitual thinking for negative, self-defeating, or worrisome thoughts. Negative thoughts will constantly fight for the steering wheel in your mind. It is your job to regain control of that steering wheel and make sure that your thoughts stay on the right road.

After really considering the things you cannot change in your life (remember, we can't change other people) it is time to refer to your other list: THINGS I CAN CHANGE from yesterday. This is where the rubber meets the road and where the real action in changing your life begins. Are you ready? This next step requires action and dedication. This next step will require you to get uncomfortable and get moving. Look at the things you have written down under the heading THINGS I CAN CHANGE. What does your first entry say? Are you unhappy with feeling alone? With being broke? With your weight? With your job or *lack* of a job? Take a *really* close look at the THINGS YOU CAN CHANGE and ask yourself the following questions: Am I *ready* to change the things in my life that I *can*? What will these changes require of me? What is the cost of *not* changing? Continued unhappiness? Continuing to be broke? Alone? Scared? Unhealthy or overweight?

Pick one item off your list of THINGS I CAN CHANGE and on a separate sheet of paper in your journal, write this thing in capital letters at the top of the page. I would now like you to list exactly what *action steps* you will take in order to change this part of your life.

For example: If your entry reads "I want to lose twenty pounds" you might come up with a list like this:

I WANT TO LOSE TWENTY POUNDS

- ⅄ I will stop eating fast food for lunch every day.
- ⅄ I will buy some healthy food options.
- ⅄ I will prepare my meals ahead of time to eliminate the excuse of "I did not have time to make meals."
- ⅄ I will begin an exercise program (if you have never exercised before, you will need to do the necessary research into different types of exercise, join a gym, or find a place in your home to exercise, somewhere to walk/jog/run, etc.)
- ⅄ I will keep a log of the types and the

amounts of food I am consuming.
- ⅄ I will weigh myself once per week.
- ⅄ I will set a "finish line" date for losing twenty pounds.

Have you noticed the wording in the *action steps*? The action steps do not say "I will *try* to stop eating fast food" or "I will *try* to make it to the grocery store to buy some healthier food options." The actions steps imply ACTION. Write your action steps for the first item off the list of THINGS I CAN CHANGE with an ABSOLUTE. What is an absolute? It is really just a promise to yourself to do something differently. Using phrases like "I will" or "I promise to" implies immediacy and importance. Remember the exercise in which I asked you to list your thoughts for an entire day? The tone and color of your thinking is incredibly important when writing your action steps. Look at how differently the following phrases sound: "Today I will go to the gym after work for one hour" versus "I will *try* my best to make it to the gym sometime today, as long as I'm not too tired, too busy with work, or asked to go out for dinner with my co-workers."

The manner in which you word your action steps will be one of the deciding factors in if you *actually begin* to take the necessary steps to change your life. When you tell yourself things like "I will stop eating fast food tomorrow as long as I get up on time to pack a lunch" you are already giving yourself an excuse to fail. You are giving yourself an "out" before you even try! MAKE SURE YOU WRITE YOUR ACTION STEPS IN ABSOLUTES.

All I ask for you to do next is to transfer *one thing* you have chosen to change off your list to the backside of your 3x5 index card from day two. You should of course include the action steps you plan on taking to change this one area of your life as well. When I need a little reminder on what I am working to change, I simply pull out my card and review my action steps to keep myself on track for the day. I also have a written record of what thoughts I want to be thinking. I can hold myself accountable wherever I am by doing these simple things. It really works.

Most importantly, write down the Serenity Prayer in its entirety (which you can find at the beginning of this book) and carry it with you always. Say it a minimum of 100 times per day. Say it slowly, to yourself or out loud, with conviction and faith. Remember that God as you understand Him is with you on this journey through change. Think of the serenity prayer as the fuel you will need to keep yourself moving as your life begins to transform. You are beginning an awesome journey into self-discovery; God will help you if you are sincerely asking for help. The only question left is this: What are you waiting for? Just begin.

Day 6

"If you really want to do something, you will find a way; if you don't, you will find an excuse" – Jim Rohn

I love this quote. This is the essence of either getting something done or finding an excuse to *not* get something done. The choice is yours.
Yesterday was a big day in your life. You took one thing in your life you have wanted to change for some time, wrote this thing down and decided how you would go about changing it by writing down action steps. You should feel accomplished, proud and motivated. If you are not quite there yet, do not worry. Today's exercise in change will help you get there, I promise!

Today we will take a close look at the *art of excuses*. Excuses are those little justifications and rationalizations that keep us from taking action in life. Consider the following statement closely: *excuses are an attempt to maximize pleasure and minimize pain.* Now say this to yourself, but use an "I" statement: *the excuses I make in life are attempts to maximize pleasure and minimize pain.* What do I mean by pain? Firstly, pain is relative. Pain is something we imagine and it exists only in the mind. I am not talking about physical pain. I am referring to something we *believe* will be painful or uncomfortable in some way. For example: if you have decided to change your exercise habits in life and get into better shape, there is only one thing stopping you from doing so – your own justifications and rationalizations. The way you are thinking about exercise is all wrong. You perceive that it will be difficult or painful in some way and your mind immediately devises a way to give you an "out". It is all too easy to get off of work, grab dinner on the way home and plop in front of the television to watch Seinfeld reruns. It would be more difficult to pack a gym bag and commit to exercising after work for an hour.

While going to the gym after work may not be actually *painful*, if it is not something you are in the habit of doing, it is minimally *uncomfortable* to change your routine. Humans resist change because it is uncomfortable. *We like to do what is easy and easy becomes a habit.* Habits can be positive or negative. If I am in the habit of going home immediately after work, sitting on my rear end and doing nothing, I have formed this habit through a series of excuses. I have gotten into the habit of justifying and rationalizing why not to exercise. Do any of these sound familiar to you? *I will start exercising once my work schedule slows down...I will make it to the gym for my New Year's resolution* (why not now?)*...I will start exercising once my wife/husband does...I will start eating a healthier diet next week...I would start exercising now, but I'm just too_____*. Read the following statement again: **the excuses I make in life are attempts to maximize pleasure and minimize pain.** Write down in your journal what excuses you might be making to avoid changing the things in your life that you can. Think about these excuses carefully. As we discussed earlier in this book, *wanting* to change and *intending* to change require just one thing…ACTION.

Benjamin Franklin said: "He that is good for making excuses is seldom good for anything else." Look at the excuses you have been making once more and finally decide to expel them from your life. You will be pleased with the results. Just begin.

Day 7

"Prepare your work outside; get everything ready for yourself in the field, and after that build your house." – Proverbs 24:27

You have been doing a lot of writing these last six days. What has this process taught you thus far? I assure you that all the hard work and effort you have put forth is leading you to the kind of life you have always imagined. The good life is not free and getting there is not easy, but I can assure you all the footwork you are putting in will be worth it.

Yesterday you began looking at your excuses - or those justifications and rationalizations - that will keep you from *changing the things you can* in your life. Today you will take the next step. Yes, it involves more writing!

One thing I have found over the years, both personally and working as an addictions professional, is the power of the written word. Most people today seem to be on auto pilot; waking up each day and doing the same things over and over. It seems that many people have forgotten how to set and achieve goals. Part of setting goals is writing them down, as you have already done. You should have chosen one area in your life in need of change and listed the steps you will take in order to *achieve* that change. You have also looked closely at the kinds of excuses you might make that will keep you from your goals.

Your life is about to get bigger, better and more focused than it has ever been.

Take the time to recreate the form on the following page. It is a Contract for Change made with *you* and it is something which warrants considerable time and effort. Whether you hand write this contract or type it, make sure it is your very best effort. I would recommend you purchase some nice quality paper and a frame for a few dollars. Why? You are going to hang this Contract for Change somewhere you will see it daily. Taking the time and effort to make a nice looking contract shows you are *serious* about changing your life. Framing it implies it is *really important* and worth protecting. Your spouse will certainly think you have gone a bit crazy. Your friends and neighbors might think you need to be in a straitjacket, but that is okay. What they think about you is *their* business, not yours!

Remember the reading from day five? Make sure you write down your goals and action steps in ABSOLUTES and remember that changing the things you can is not rocket science. Do not over complicate simple ideas. Your goals for personal change do not have to be life shattering, earth moving changes. Your goals for change could be as simple as getting up 30 minutes earlier to get to work on time, going for a walk, or keeping your house clean and orderly. Remember *it is okay to start with small steps. All the small steps you take towards a larger goal really add up.* If your goal is to enroll in a college course, you might start by researching the local community college offerings. You might set an appointment with a career counselor or set up an appointment to visit campus. Remember, *there is great power in taking action, no matter how small the action is.* All you must do is begin.

PERSONAL CONTRACT FOR CHANGE

I, _____ have decided to take
action on the following part(s) of my life today
(date) _____:

1) _____
_____
_____

2) _____
_____
_____

3) _____
_____
_____

4) _____
_____
_____

5) _____
_____
_____

I have decided to take action on the above items
because I am tired of living a life of complacency.
I have committed to making these changes now. I
will not wait. I will not find an excuse to do what I
need to do. Today I will live in the solution and
not the problem.

Signed: _____

Chop Wood.

Carry Water.

Repeat.

Day 8

What is not growing is dying. My wife and I live on a beautiful piece of heavily wooded property in Michigan. Our property is full of lodge pole pines, oaks trees, birch trees, ash trees and all sorts of ferns and wild flowers. We even have a family of turkeys that like to call our woods home. It is not uncommon to see deer, owls and coyotes on any given day. It is really quite beautiful and I feel blessed to be able to call this chunk of land home.

Part of living in the woods in Michigan is dealing with the Emerald Ash Borer Beetle or *Agrilus Planipennis.* These little beetles wreak havoc on Ash Trees, sucking them dry of valuable nutrients and essentially starving the trees from the inside out. I have lost several trees this year alone, many of them quite close to my home. It is often necessary for me to remove the dead trees so they do not cause any damage to my property. Although I hate cutting down any tree, sometimes *I have to do what I do not want to do.*

Thank God for my trusty new chainsaw, my love of using it and my need for firewood. Thankfully no ash tree has gone to waste just yet. Once I have cut a dead tree down, I can chop it up for firewood to burn in my shop. There is a state-wide quarantine on the Ash tree. An infested tree cannot be moved to another location for fear that the little beetles will find new homes. You probably had not intended on receiving a lesson on tree botany, had you? What does all this talk about trees and beetles have to do with you? Consider again the quotation from Carlos Castaneda: *"We hardly ever realize that we can cut anything out of our lives, anytime, in the blink of an eye."*

What areas of your life are infecting your happiness and serenity? What areas do you need to chop down, cut out and remove before the infestation becomes worse? Are things like too much T.V., toxic relationships, fast food, pornography, video games, smoking, drinking, gambling, spending money you do not have, too much or too little sleep, gossip, or procrastination infesting the good, *healthy* parts of your life? I can answer this for you: YES THEY ARE.

Begin at once to remove the sick and unhealthy parts of your life, one at a time. Consider how these unhealthy parts of your life have limited your true potential. Write about it. Pray about it. No matter how you decide to take action, sharpen your saws and *get cutting*.

A simple program

for complicated

people.

<u>Day 9</u>

"Life is really simple, but we insist on making it complicated." – Confucius

Yesterday you began thinking about the parts of your life that are infected and unhealthy. You began to cut these things or behaviors of your life out, one by one. This is a practice which will continue into today, tomorrow, next week and hopefully for the rest of your life. Keep cutting out the infected parts of your life so the healthy parts can grow big, strong and beautiful. On to the next lesson.

Do you want to know what a person's life is *really* like? Here is a sure-fire way to know. Firstly, do not listen to what they say. Talk is cheap. Instead, *watch what they do* (more on this later.) Secondly, look at how a person keeps their belongings: the condition of their home or personal space, their vehicle, their yard and so on. Do you see excessive "stuff" everywhere? What about in your own life? Do your hoard things? Do you always tell yourself "I will use this or that someday" but never do? Do you take care of what you have? Your home? Your car? Your clothing? What does this say about you?

Because I am an appropriate case study in my own right, I will use myself as an example. Some lessons are learned the hard way; for me, this was certainly one of them. My wife loving tells me "Honey, you are so OCD! You are so anal about your stuff!" She is right, I am. This is why: keeping things neat and orderly in my life breeds neat and orderly thoughts. Neat and orderly thoughts breed healthy emotions. As we have already learned, healthy emotions breed positive and constructive actions. Positive and constructive actions produce good results.

For years and years I felt like Pigpen from the cartoon *Snoopy*. Everywhere I went, everywhere I lived, the vehicles I drove and my surroundings in general were complete and total disasters. I could never find my keys, my wallet, bills and so on. During this period of complete and utter chaos, I was living a life fueled by drugs, alcohol and immediate gratification. Many years ago, part of my journey into becoming a responsible recovering person was learning to take care of myself and my surroundings.

My Grandmother or "Baba" always used to say "soap and water don't cost much." This is coming from a woman who had very little, but knew a faith and a peace like I had never known before. Baba and Papa (my Grandfather) raised six children in a small home in Wyandotte, MI. They drove vehicles in various states of disrepair and they rarely had money to spend on themselves. My Papa, a World War II veteran, worked multiple jobs to support his family, with most of his earnings spent on putting food on the table. One thing I remember about their home was how proud they were of it. Papa did all of the remodeling and repairs himself and his work was flawless. And though small and sparsely furnished, their home was always immaculate. Even their tiny yard looked like a picture from *Better Homes & Gardens*. Baba's flowers were beautiful. Papa kept the lawn neatly mowed and the sidewalk swept. Baba did not have excessive clutter everywhere (Papa's garage, or the *Holy Grail* to all the grandchildren, was a different story entirely.) What they *did* have they took care of. *Soap and water don't cost much, Paul.* I can still hear her saying that today.

I encourage you to take an honest assessment of the clutter that has built up in your life. What can you get rid of? Give to charity? Do you know someone personally that might need some of your "stuff?" Just how many pairs of shoes do you need? Start today and consider how you keep your surroundings – at home, at work and all of your personal belongings – and ask yourself if you really need all this *stuff*. A simple life is a good life. *Happiness is wanting what you already have;* taking care of it and being grateful for it.

Take one area of your life today (it is okay to start small, say with the junk drawer in the kitchen) and take a look at the clutter in your life. Get rid of what you do not use and take care of what you choose to keep. All you must do is begin.

I can't.

GOD CAN.

I think I'll let Him.

Day 10

"You cannot escape the responsibility of tomorrow by evading it today"
– *Abraham Lincoln*

Proverbs 20:4 states *"The sluggard does not plow in the autumn; he will seek at harvest and have nothing."* Anything that is written in the Bible I take as law and this short yet simple idea from Proverbs is no exception. Procrastination is the thief of time, dreams and happiness.

Procrastination causes us unnecessary anxiety and is like living life on the deferment plan. Honestly ask yourself this: *what have you been putting off that needs to be done?* We all have "to do" lists, things we need to get done *now* and things that are not as urgent. What kinds of things on your "to do" list have been dominating your thoughts lately? What has kept you from working to accomplish these things? Do you not believe these things are possible? Do you tell yourself "I just don't have the time right now" or "I will do_____ when _____." Think about how you have been spending your time lately. How much of your day is spent surfing the internet? Just how much T.V. do you watch? Is there a way you could spend your time differently? I am sure that there is. We are all guilty of avoiding the things in life that must be done, especially the things we do not wish to do.

As we have already explored earlier in this devotional, *justifying and rationalizing are the enemies of action*. The following exercise is by no means new, nor is it anything terribly complicated. Just as I have asked you to take an honest self-assessment of your thoughts, I would now ask that you take an honest assessment of your time.

At the top of a page in your journal, neatly write down the top five things you have been putting off in life (and start with the most undesirable task first.) For the rest of the day, I would ask that you write down how you have spent each waking hour. Keep this up for the next several days, or as long as you choose to do so. From the time that you roll out of bed in the morning until the time you lay down at night, do your very best to account for every single minute. You will be surprised how much time you spend doing nothing: watching television, playing on your smartphone, grazing in the kitchen, or gossiping about others. Just imagine if you dedicated thirty minutes a day to getting the number one thing on your list done. Where would you be in a week? A month? A year?

This is a concept I practice in my own life. Once I began graduate school, I found it difficult to come home and concentrate on research after working all day. I have somewhat of a short attention span and I downright refuse to sit in front of a computer when the sun is shining in the afternoon. So in order to work towards my goal of completing my master's degree, I began to wake up early each morning. How early? 3 or 4 a.m. early. Was this hard at first? You bet it was. Instead of getting up at six, watching the news and drinking coffee for an hour, I began getting up just a few minutes earlier each week and chipped away at the pile of school work that waited for me each morning on my desk. I employed the same tactic for getting to the gym each morning for workouts.

You may not be a morning person and that is okay. ***We are each given the exact same number of hours each day and it is up to us how we use them.*** How will you use your time today? Starting *now*, take a careful look at how you are spending your time. You will find that there are plenty of hours in the day for you to do what must be done. Time management is a discipline. It is a choice. ***Begin today to become a master of your time. Do not make time a master of you.***

Day 11

"Never limit your view of life by any past experience" – Ernest Holmes

What are you afraid of? How have your fears limited your ability to live your life to the fullest? Think about this carefully. Most of the things that we fear will happen *never do happen*. Our minds work just like the processor in a computer – they store data. Your brain has multiple jobs, a few of which are storing experiences: past experiences, beliefs and feelings, along with processing what is happening in your world *right now*, just to name a few. All of your past experiences make you who you are today. So just who *are* you today? What kinds of messages did you hear as a child? Were they positive, affirming messages like *I believe in you* or *you can do this* or maybe even *you are good enough just the way you are*? Did you ever receive harmful messages?

Were you ever told that you *could not do something?* I certainly was. I began getting in with the wrong crowd at a very young age. I made some very irresponsible choices as a kid. As a result of the unhealthy choices I made, I began to receive very particular kinds of messages from teachers, coaches and probation officers: *you will never amount to anything…college is not for everyone…you are going to end up in prison or dead!* After hearing these types of messages long enough, I began believing what the adults in my life were telling me: *maybe I can't go to college...maybe I'm not going to amount to much...maybe what everyone is telling me is true!*

The fancy term for what I am describing to you is a *Schema*, taken from *Schema Therapy* developed by Dr. Jeffery E. Young. In essence, a Schema is a set of beliefs one has about oneself; they are preconceived ways of thinking or behaving that correspond with early childhood experiences. Think back to your childhood and recall what kinds of messages you received from others. What was your life like as a young person? Do you remember any traumatic or disturbing experiences? The definitions of *traumatic* or *disturbing* will vary from person to person; because of course experience is largely subjective.

How are some of the beliefs you held about yourself as a child still playing out in your life today? Are you nervous in new social situations? Are you afraid to try new things? Do you still have issues with authority figures? What about with the opposite sex? Is it difficult to stand up for yourself, be assertive and say what needs to be said? I would ask that you devote a minimum of twenty minutes today and journal about what you experienced as a child. Go into as much or as little detail as you would like. The Greek philosopher Epictetus said that "We are disturbed not by what happens to us, but by our thoughts about what happens." How are your beliefs limiting you? Are you still a slave to the lies you were told early in life? Think about this and remember: All you must do is begin.

Day 12

"The cave you fear to enter holds the treasure you seek" – Joseph Campbell

Going to college was something I had always wanted to do but never gave myself *permission* to do. For the vast majority of my life, I subscribed to the belief that I just was not college material. I kept this belief alive by consistently doubting my ability to return to school, making excuses and never giving myself a chance to succeed. When I lived in Colorado, I worked as a diesel mechanic and welder. These were professions I was really good at and jobs I enjoyed, but I always wanted something different in my life. Sure, turning wrenches and welding steel are very noble and highly skilled professions, but after getting sober, I lost the spark for doing this type of work. I had firmly planted in the back of my mind *what if I could go to college? What would it be like? Would I even be able to get in?* I like to think that questions like these are nudges from God to make a move, so I did.

What I found out about college was that you just cannot go sign up. They want to see your grades from high school. They even make you write an essay about *why* you want to go to college. They ask you to sign up for classes and they also make you pay for those classes. I found that going to college would be a lot more work than I had ever bargained for. First, I had to take a few classes at community college in order to establish a positive academic record (no one would admit me having barely made it through high school.) Second, I would need to figure out what I wanted to study. Third, I would need to buy a computer and figure out how to use it. Lastly, I would need to navigate how to work a full time job and still make it onto campus every day. I had my work cut out for me, but *all I needed to do was begin to work in the direction of my goal. All I had to do was begin.*

When I finally got accepted into a college I could barely contain my excitement. I remember my first day of classes like it was yesterday. I had worked hard to get to this point, but I was terrified at what the day might bring. I felt as if I was back in kindergarten all over again, back to the first day of school. Back to attending "special" classes, back to struggling with my work, to wondering if I could make it through the day. *I literally felt like I was five years old again.* My schemas, or *the beliefs I had about myself,* school, and my academic abilities all came rushing back.

Here I was, in my mid-twenties, in a sea of 18 and 19 year olds. I could not find a place to park. I could not find my first class. I did not realize how big a university campus actually was. I had a backpack packed with books and a shiny new laptop I did not even know how to use. I felt as if all the "kids" walking to class everywhere were staring at me, wondering "what is he doing here?" I certainly did not fit the profile of a college freshman: older, bald, heavily tattooed and wearing greasy boots from work because I had somehow forgotten to pack a pair of shoes. I was scared, to say the least, trying to navigate my way around the campus that day.

I was a guy who was proud to say he was not afraid of *anything*. In my active addiction, I frequented many places that I would not wish my worst enemy to go to. I hung out in dangerous places, did dangerous things and lived life with fearless attitude. I was not afraid of *anybody* or *anything* – so I thought.

Getting clean and sober taught me that it is okay to be afraid, but it is *not* okay to let fear paralyze you. It is not okay to let your fears limit what you can and cannot do in life. I like to think of fear as *False Evidence Appearing Real.* **FEAR** is really just our own estimation of what *could* happen, what *might* happen and how we *might* respond. **FEAR** is based on past events and experiences in our lives.

Have you ever watched a little boy play? It brings me great joy to spend time with my little nephews and even greater joy to watch them play. They are innocent and uncorrupted. My youngest nephew, Jake, is a little tank. Jake is fearless. When he jumps on the bed, rides his bike, or plays "pirate" with his brother Sean, he does not worry about getting hurt, getting judged, or about what other people might think. Jake does not worry about *what if I trip and sprain my ankle? What if I try and ride my bike and I fall? What if I try playing catch and I'm no good at it?* Jake does not think in these ways because his mind is not filled with past failures, traumatic events and limiting beliefs about himself. He lives *in* the moment and lives *for* the moment. If he wants to do something, he just does it (under my sister Carrie's watchful eye.) Failure for Jake is not an option, because he does not yet know the *meaning* of failure or FEAR.

Ask yourself the following, and write about it in your journal: How are your fears holding you back from taking the necessary steps to realize your goals and dreams? Where did these fears originate? What if you could live your life like little Jake does – a life without fear, judgment, or limiting beliefs? What would your life be like if you gave yourself *permission* to try the thing you fear the most? Consider these questions carefully. Do something you are afraid to do today. Do something that is outside of your comfort zone. Remember this: It is okay to start small. Just begin.

Day 13

"Life is either a daring adventure, or it is nothing" – Helen Keller

If you have put in the work thus far, you should be viewing yourself and your reality much differently by now. You have really begun to look at your life in the past twelve days. I hope by this point you are feeling better about where you are *now* and where you are *going*.

Yesterday you examined your fears and limiting beliefs. We can talk all day, every day, about what we are *going* to do. I am *going* to go back to school someday. I am *going* to ask that special someone for their phone number. I am *going* to sign up for that exercise class. I am *going* to take that trip. What is stopping you? Maybe you feel that life has gotten a bit bland. Maybe you are thinking *there has to be more to life than this*. Maybe you are just plain bored and dissatisfied with the same activities, day in and day out. *The problem is that you have gotten too comfortable with your current reality.*

When is the last time you tried something new? When is the last time you felt truly excited about something? If it is hard for you to recall *ever* feeling excited about your life, read on. If you feel like you are in a slump, read on. Even if you simply want to challenge yourself to make life just that much better, by all means read on.

Remember that the only thing keeping you from trying something new and *making life a daring adventure* is the way you are thinking. *Starting today, ask yourself what parts of your life have become stagnant.* Ask yourself what you can do, *starting now*, to change those parts of your life.

Do you know what happens to a pond without a fresh supply of water running into it? You guessed it. The pond becomes stagnant, black and begins to smell. Without a way for the pond to constantly replenish its fresh water supply, the life it holds begins to die. The pond begins to dry up. All living things need a constant supply of water in order to sustain themselves, in order to remain healthy and in order to grow. Does your pond have a fresh, healthy supply of water feeding it, or has your pond begun to dry up? What does you pond look like today and what are you willing to do to change it? Eleanor Roosevelt said "The purpose of life is to live it, to taste experience to the utmost, to reach out eagerly and without fear for newer and richer experience."

So what are you waiting for? If your life has become a dried up pond, if life has become stagnant, do something differently. START NOW. All you must do is begin.

Easy does it.

BUT DO IT.

Day 14

"A smooth sea never made a skilled sailor"
– English Proverb

Life is hard. Once you accept this fact, life *can* and *will* get easier. Remember one of our earlier readings about acceptance? If you are having trouble remembering just what acceptance means, go back and read the devotional for Day 3. If you are continuing to work on *accepting the things you cannot change* and are also working to *change the things you can*, you are probably finding that change is not comfortable, easy and things do not always go as planned. If things are not going your way, rejoice, because you are growing!

Imagine for a second if everything you ever planned to do, everything you wanted and everything you worked for turned out just how you had expected. Imagine if things always went your way. Sound good? I can assure you that it is not. If you believe for one second that you are the one running the show, calling the shots and controlling the outcomes of your actions, you are wrong. You are terribly wrong and this is why: God is in control. Read this again: GOD IS IN CONTROL.

Do you not believe this is true? Think about this: have things *always* gone as you have planned? Have you *always* gotten your way? Do you spend countless hours, days, weeks, months and years planning for what *you* want to do? Think about all the times in your life that you have hit a rough patch – lost a job, a loved one, fallen ill, or unexpectedly found yourself in a situation you never could have planned for. How do you explain such things? I will tell you – you can't. Some things in life simply cannot be explained. Those areas are God's business and His alone.

Here is the good news: GOD IS IN CHARGE OF WORRY AND YOU ARE IN CHARGE OF WORK. When tough times hit – and they will – be grateful. Have faith that *nothing* is happening in your life that God did not plan for. It is when life is most difficult that we are growing, changing, learning and becoming stronger individuals. It is through hardships that we can become closer to God as we understand Him.

Remember again the reading on acceptance. True acceptance means really knowing the reality of a situation, without attempting to change, escape, or evade it. As it is often muttered in recovery circles, acceptance is saying *it is what it is* and being okay with that. Without some measure of pain we cease growing. If we are not thrown the occasional curveball in life, we can easily become disillusioned to believe that we are the ones in control. Accept hardships as part of your life. Life is not supposed to be easy and it is rarely supposed to make sense. Let God worry and keep on working, no matter how hard life may get. All you must do is keep moving forward.

You are

EXACTLY

Where you are

Supposed to be

RIGHT NOW.

Day 15

"Expectations minus reality equals disappointment" – Dr. Randy Carlson

If you have come to the realization that God is in charge of worry and you are in charge of work, congratulations. You have made an authentic first step into living life on life's terms, one day at a time. You learned yesterday that hardships in life are really just part of the journey. Much of human suffering can be traced back to *expectations*. Expectations for how things *should* be, how someone *should* treat us, how our children *should* act, how far in life we *should* be, how our finances, our health, or our relationships *should* look and so on.

Close your eyes for a moment and imagine the last time you were upset. You do not have to have been boiling over, red-zone angry. Just upset. Think of *why* you were upset. I am not a mind reader, but I have a pretty good idea of the source of your disappointment: **you expected something to go a certain way and it did not. You expected to be treated a certain way and you were not.**

Expectations can rob you of the current moment. They can keep us from living life to its fullest. After all, life is happening *right now*. This is it. This is what you have got, sitting or standing wherever you are, reading this book. THIS IS IT. Are you daydreaming about how your plans will turn out? My bet is that you are. We are all guilty of this in some way. Are you planning excessively for your future and think that you have things all sorted out? I am sure that on some level, you do. What if your plans do not turn out the way you expected? What if someone you expect to treat you with kindness and respect treats you otherwise? If things do not go as you had planned, will it ruin your day? Will you secretly harbor resentments and stew about what *could* have been, how you *should* have been treated, or about how life is not fair? These are questions which should not be taken lightly.

What if, for a change, you did not expect anything? I am in no way saying that you should not live your life with hope, passion and faith for better things to come. I am merely suggesting that you attempt to get into the practice of NOT EXPECTING ANY PARTICULAR OUTCOME.

Surrender the RESULTS of your planning and hard work to God. Let him be the one who decides how things will turn out in your life. *Expect that things will happen unexpectedly*. Expect that you will find yourself in situations you never dreamed possible. Think of your biggest dream. Think of what it would feel like to live that dream. GOD IS DREAMING BIGGER. He knows what you need before you even need it, so stop worrying, stop expecting things to go your way and accept life as it happens. Just for today.

Coincidence is God's

Way of

Staying Anonymous.

Day 16

"If God is your co-pilot you are in the wrong seat!" – Unknown

Any 12-step program involves an admission of powerlessness over one's dependencies. On top of that, we realize that *we are not the ones in control* of our own lives. God is in control. How can this be, you ask? You might be thinking: *I am in perfect control of my life. I am in control of what I do, what I say, where I work, how I spend my money and how I spend my time.* While this may be true - because God gave us free will, after all - you are *not* in control of outcomes. You are *not* in control of the future. ***You are only in control of what you think and what you do.***

As you read yesterday, expectations can be a very dangerous thing. Expectations can cause unnecessary anxiety, worry and disappointment. They can lead us to destructive feelings: anger, resentment, depression, anxiety, bitterness, shame and guilt. If you have begun to realize that God is in charge of worrying about the future and you are in charge of doing the work that must be done *today*, you are continuing on a path which leads to serenity and peace.

I have often seen bumper stickers that read GOD IS MY CO-PILOT. While this is a novel concept, it is wrong. God is the PILOT, we are the passengers. Part of the problem with most people today is that they continuously try to manipulate the variables in their lives so that things can happen *their own way*. They think they know better than God, better than the One who created them. You have probably found in your own life that the more you try and force something, the harder it seems to get: be that with a relationship, finances, career, your health, or just about anything else for that matter. The bumper sticker should read I AM GOD'S CO-PILOT.

When was the last time you flew on a big commercial airliner? Do you remember boarding the plane and walking past the pilot? He probably greeted you and said "enjoy your flight" or something similar. Once all the passengers have found their seats and stowed their luggage, the plane is sealed shut and takes off towards its destination.

You are putting your *absolute trust* and *faith* into a pilot you have probably only met for a spilt second, if at all. The pilot sits in the cockpit behind a locked door and has the difficult task of getting the passengers to their destination safely. The pilot has all the skills and expertise he needs; the coordinates of where he is going and all the instrumentation he needs to help get him get there. He does not need your help! It would be insane (and it would get you into all kinds of trouble these days) for you to get up out of your seat, go knock on the cockpit door and ask *"Excuse me, Mr. Pilot, are you sure you know where you are going?*

Although I have never flown a plane, would you like me to take over the controls for you?"

How often do you do this in your own life? When things are not going how you think they should be going, do you take back the controls of your life and start steering your plane again? What usually happens? Well, if you are anything like me, you usually end up in trouble of some sort. The "plane" of life gets off course and things fall apart. Stop taking over the controls. ***Stop telling God what he should do and let Him do His job.*** Trust God with everything and He will get you to your destination.

Day 17

"Things don't change, only the way you look at them" – Carlos Castaneda

What Carlos Castaneda is describing has been written about since Biblical times – changing the way we think. Review again your thought log from day one and ask yourself again, today, what the general tone of your thinking has been. Things in your life may not be perfect, but remember that the one thing you *can* change, *right now*, is the manner in which you think.

I personally love the winter season, but I know several people that *despise* it. We will use winter in Michigan as an example to prove how powerful our thoughts can be. Assume that you are one of those people who do not like winter. You do not like the cold, the icy roads, or shoveling snow. You do not like to get up extra early to scrape off your car, bundling up in a heavy winter coat and dislike being cooped up indoors for six months. Fair enough. It is your choice to dislike winter.

Assume that upon awakening each winter morning your first conscious thoughts are *oh boy, it is going to be a long, cold day. I hate winter. It is dark when I drive to work and dark when I drive home from work. I cannot stand the cold. I am going to have to bundle up to go scrape off my car and if it snows today I will have to dig out the snow blower. What a pain!* Whether you know it or not, you have already set the tone for how your day will go. If you are constantly thinking about how much you hate winter, you will probably complain about it to your co-workers. They will likely feed into your complaining and even join in. Your pessimistic attitude will feed your behaviors throughout the day as well. A pessimistic, negative attitude breeds self-defeating, negative actions.

Because of your negative attitude, you might forgo getting to a 12-step meeting, getting to the gym, or getting together with friends. You might be thinking *I just want this day to end...it is so cold outside; all I want to do is get home, click on the television and relax.* Again, that is your choice. Choosing not to be an active participant in your own life just because it is dark and cold – choosing to live your life as a victim – is *again* your own choice. Living life this way breeds rationalization and justification (remember these words? They are the enemy) and will produce more negative thoughts and negative actions. Days and weeks go by, and you begin to think *Boy, I have not been getting anything done! I just feel so lazy during the winter. I have put on some weight and I have been feeling so depressed! Once spring comes, I will start participating in my own life again...but not until then! It is just too dreary and cold!*

Believe it or not, you are choosing the way you feel by the way you think about winter. You have made it okay for you to "check out" of life, to not handle your responsibilities and you are feeling lazy and guilty because of these choices. You have decided to become a bystander in your own life. The way you are thinking about winter has been the spark which ignited the fire which burns with negativity.

Just imagine how differently your day would go if upon awakening, you *decided* to think in the following manner: *Thank you, God, for waking me up this morning! It is going to be a great day. I might have to get up and scrape off my car, but I am so grateful to have a car to scrape off! I am thankful to have a job to go to. I am thankful that I have a driveway to shovel. I am thankful that I have a warm winter coat to wear. Michigan is such a beautiful place in the winter. Even though it is cold, I will make my best effort to do something outside, even for a few minutes. I have plenty of things I can do to occupy myself and be an active participant in my own life. How today goes is up to me and me alone and I plan to make this a great day!*

Sound a bit far-fetched, maybe even a little cheesy? Do you doubt that just thinking differently will improve your life that much? Guess what? *It will.* Look for the positives in life and you will find more things to be thankful for. Look for the negatives in life and you will only find more negatives. Try this just for today. All you must do is begin.

Day 18

"Change your thoughts and you change your world" – Norman Vincent Peale

We have spent considerable time thus far looking at the way that we think. Changing the tone of your habitual thinking is the one thing that can begin to change your life for the better starting *today*. Life is pure perception. Shakespeare said that "Nothing in life is good or bad but thinking makes it so." Take, for example, the dreaded Monday morning. For years and years I absolutely hated Monday mornings. Monday mornings meant a return to the grind; back to work, back to dealing with people and problems. Back to fighting traffic, paying bills, cooking dinner, getting to bed early and so on. As you read yesterday, if I attach a negative thought to some person, place, or thing, I will have a negative reaction *emotionally*. A negative emotion can only produce a negative *action* or *behavior* and negative actions or behaviors will only produce negative *results*.

I challenge you to pick one part of your life today and work on changing the way you think about it. Remember this: WE ARE WHAT WE THINK. If you think over and over again *I love Mondays! It means the start of a new week and a chance to work on improving myself. It means I have been given one more chance at this journey called life* you are choosing your attitude. This is the most powerful choice you can make each day: A

POSITIVE ATTITUDE.

If you begin to change the way you think about Mondays, or any other area of your life for that matter, you will begin to feel differently. You will begin to act differently and of course the results of your actions will change as well. Think back to day two when you began looking at your *thought diet.* Carefully analyze what you are feeding your mentality today, just for a refresher. Are you feeding it jealous thoughts? Victim thoughts? Thoughts about lack, worry, or fear?

What if you were to change the way you thought about *just one* area of your life, *starting today* and changed this thought for good? Do you think you could keep this up for an entire day? What about an entire week? Try this exercise to help you: pick one area of your life you view as problematic and change the thoughts attached to it. I find in incredibly helpful to use sticky notes for this exercise. Write down *alternate positive thoughts* to replace the *negative thoughts* you have attached to this area of your life on several sticky notes and place them where you will see them. It is helpful to place them in areas of your home, office, or car where you will be *forced* to look at them. I put one on the bathroom mirror, one on the dashboard of my vehicle and affix one to my computer monitor at work. Every single time that a negative thought pops into your head, *immediately* disregard it and think the positive thought instead. It sounds too simple to actually work, but it does! Try it today.

RIGHT NOW

You already have

EVERYTHING

You need to CHANGE.

GET BUSY.

Day 19

"Do what you can, with what you have, where you are at" – Theodore Roosevelt

Are you living your life in the future? Do you believe that once you are financially secure, own your own home, or buy a new car you will then be happy? When you live in a nice neighborhood? When you have your dream job? Do you ever put any disclaimers on being happy? I WILL BE HAPPY WHEN_____. This is surely no way to live your life, but it is a fact that this is how most people operate today.

We live in a world of excess and lethargy. Supersize fast food meals. SUV's with 60,000 dollar price tags. Online shopping with next day delivery. Internet access, instant messaging, texting and email at the touch of a button. Paying other people to do the things we can easily do ourselves – mowing our lawns, shoveling our snow, even picking up after our pets. When you put a *condition* on happiness, you will NEVER BE HAPPY. You will never be content with *what is*, because you will be constantly thinking about *what could be*. Once I get my promotion. Once I find my calling in life. Once I am married. Once I am out of debt. Once I am thin. The list goes on indefinitely.

In no way am I suggesting that you should settle for living a mediocre, hum-drum existence. I am not suggesting that you simply say "this is all I will ever achieve, all I will ever have and all I will ever be." NO! ABSOLUTELY NOT THE CASE. What I *am* suggesting is that you learn to *do what you can, with what you have, where you are at* TODAY. Today is part of your journey into tomorrow. Do your best to be grateful for what you have RIGHT NOW. Live with expectancy that things will get better if you are trying to live your life the way you believe God wants you to. Trust that you have everything you need to be healthy, happy and successful *right now.* You do. It is just a matter of learning how to use what you already have to your benefit.

Happiness means wanting what you already have. Do not focus so much on material things. Material things come and go. Think about your abilities, your talents and your blessings. Think about the mere fact that you are alive and well enough to be reading this. Think about the fact that you have a choice in your attitude. You have a choice how to spend your time. You have a choice what you think about.

In your journal write out a list of things you are grateful for today and keep it with you at all times. Refer to this list whenever you begin to feel sorry for yourself, whenever you become jealous, spiteful, or depressed. Thinking about just how good you have it RIGHT NOW is a great way to be happy. A positive attitude costs nothing. Start today. All you must do is begin.

What isn't

GROWING

Is

DYING.

Day 20

"A ship is safe in harbor, but that's not what ships are for." – William G.T. Shedd

Television is a formidable opponent, and it is one of humankind's sneakiest enemies today. Untold numbers of hours are spent by people every day starring at an electronic box, watching images of other people participating in life.

With more cable channels than ever, it is quite possible to click on the old idiot box and "tune in" to watch people in all sorts of situations: a bunch of strangers living in a house together (we call this entertainment?); a group of people living on an island, attempting to survive (with film crews close by, of course); "celebrity news" type programs, which catch us up on the latest Hollywood gossip (who cares?); and my personal favorite topping the list would have to be the "police" type shows, in which millions of viewers can sit comfortably in their favorite chairs, sipping a cold beverage, all while watching complete strangers at possibly the worst moments of their lives. I have always found the "police" genre of programming to be a real indication of humanity today. We take pleasure – we even call it *entertainment* – to watch other people suffer. Watching women get beaten, children taken from their parents, gang members shooting at one another and homeless individuals getting harassed for being homeless. It is all too easy to sit in the comfort of our own homes, eyes glued to the newest sixty-inch flat screen T.V. and watch life happen.

The lives we live have become too safe. Watching too much T.V. is not *tuning in*, it is actually *tuning out*. We have become a sedentary, complacent society. We have become too dependent on media to provide us thrills and adventure in life. It is a sad reality, but one that is true.

Life begins right outside your comfort zone. Those seven little words are game changers. Do you like to travel? What about instead of watching endless hours of travel programming on T.V., you took a trip? Don't have the money? You can always start small. Go explore a town near your home, learn about its history and chat with the locals. Do you like to cook? Or would you *like to know* how to cook? What if instead of watching show after cooking show, you found a recipe and tried preparing it as a surprise to your spouse or best friend? Have you ever seen the countless "get ripped, get buff, lose fifty pounds in thirty days" commercials? What if instead of watching other people exercise, you got up off your comfortable couch and got moving? Not next week, not as a New Year's resolution, but TODAY. If you have become bored in life, it is because you have become too comfortable. If you do not like the way you feel, do something different. All you must do is begin.

Day 21

"You will find the key to success under the alarm clock" – Benjamin Franklin

WAKE UP! Now is the time for you to get started doing whatever it is you want to do in life. When I was newly sober and my eyes were *really* open to the reality and possibilities of life for the first time, I often wondered how people became so successful. I had been living in a perpetual fog fueled by whiskey and drugs since I was in junior high school and because of the choices I made, I failed to learn many of the lessons life had to teach me. Sure, I learned plenty of lessons about breaking the law and suffering the consequences: lessons about the amounts of whiskey and narcotics my body could handle, lessons about fear, desperation and death. What I failed to learn was how to set a goal and work towards it. I learned this lesson well – and continue learning it – through recovery and hard work.

I used to look at other men my age who had rewarding careers, drove nice cars and took vacations to warm and sunny places. I comforted myself by thinking *Oh, their parents must have been rich, or they must have just gotten lucky...they must have gotten a break.* While this may be the case in *some* situations, the vast majority of people who are living productive, successful and happy lives have worked their tails off. There is no substitute for hard work. There are no freebies and there no shortcuts. Just work. Lots of hard work.

I vividly remember sitting at training in Cambridge, Massachusetts early in my career as an addiction professional. I had just been rewarded entry into a four-year college and had been hired as an intern at a counseling agency. My supervisor really believed in me. She believed in me so much that she sent me to a four-day training on domestic violence and co-occurring mental health disorders. I sat in a room with some very distinguished individuals: medical doctors, attorneys, psychologists and university professors.

Then there was me. I was a new to playing dress-up to go to work. My usual work apparel up to that point consisted of a pair of coveralls with my name sewn on the front pocket, steel toed work boots, a welding hood and a pocket full of wrenches - complete with grease under my fingernails that never seemed to go away. Mingling with the upper echelon of society was a brand new and scary prospect for me. I had been to some *very* scary and intimidating places in my life, but this took the cake. That, in my opinion, is where God intervened.

I was feeling self-conscious in my newly purchased dress pants, button down shirt and tie from one of those "discount" type stores. I was not even used to tucking in my shirt. I had not even *owned* a dress shirt up to this point. I walked into the hotel where the training was being held and found my seat next to a very grandmotherly looking African American woman, probably in her late seventies. When I said earlier that God intervened, this is what I meant: the woman introduced herself and asked me my name. *My name is Paul*, I said. She asked me what discipline I was in. *What discipline?* She looked at me kindly and chuckled. "What I mean, sweetie, is what line of work you are in? What brings you here? What is your educational background?" *Um…I'm an intern at a counseling agency in Michigan, and I go to Central Michigan University.* "Oh, how lovely. Which doctoral program are you in? Psychology?" I was confused at her question. *Doctoral program? I'm not in any doctoral program. I'm in my first semester of college. I didn't start school until much later in life…I took a different path, I guess.*

I figured she was some well-known doctor or educator and I was embarrassed that I did not even have three college credits under my belt. She seemed to sense this and said "Oh honey, good for you. I can see that you feel uncomfortable. You don't hide it well. I get the sense that you've lived a pretty hard life…I don't know what gives me that feeling, but I get that from you." I sipped my drink and mustered up the courage to ask her what she did for a living. That *is* what "normal" people do in these types of situations, isn't it? So I opened my mouth and asked "So, what about you? What do you do?" Her answer floored me.

She basically told me her entire life story. She was the youngest of eleven children and was raised on a farm in a tiny town in southern Alabama. Her father was a raging alcoholic who administered regular beatings to her and her older siblings. Her mother suffered from a variety of serious mental disorders and had spent most of her life confined to mental institutions, jails and prisons. This delicate old woman was a recovering alcoholic herself who had raised five kids of her own. During her drinking days, she said she regularly worked three or four waitressing jobs at a time to afford her alcohol, put food on the table and keep the lights on. Her five children all grew up to be healthy, successful individuals.

What really got me was this: for the last twenty years since getting sober, she had been working on her college degree. *Twenty years?* Yes, you read that correctly. *Twenty years.* She worked at a Community Mental Health agency somewhere in Indiana as a receptionist. Her dream job was to one day become a therapist and help those who could not help themselves. She refused to take out college loans and only took classes when she could afford to. But she never gave up. I said something along the lines of *wow, that's impressive!* Her reply? "Not really, honey. I just trust my God and put in the work. Do you know how you eat an elephant? One bite at a time!"

Her story is a testament to hard work, dedication, perseverance and patience. The good life ain't free.

You must work for it. Her story is one that I was meant to hear at that *exact* moment in my life. I'm not patting myself on the back, nor am I looking for high-fives or accolades. I share this part of my life with you because someone shared a piece of their life with me, *exactly* when I needed it the most.

So what are you waiting for? The elephant will not eat itself. What do you dream of doing the most? Are you willing to take the path less traveled to get there, even if it takes you twenty years? Good! The best news of all is that all you must do is begin.

Day 22

"You have brains in your head. You have feet in your shoes. You can steer yourself any direction you choose. You're on your own. And you know what you know. And YOU are the one who'll decide where to go." – Dr. Seuss

Life is nothing more than a series of choices. All of the choices you have made so far in life have brought you to the EXACT point where you are today. As you have already learned, doing good makes you feel good and doing bad makes you feel bad. Let us concentrate on making good choices and taking ACTION above all else.

Do you remember the difference between a *successful* person and an *unsuccessful* person? In a word, WORK. Do you spend more time complaining about what you do not have than you do working to get it? In counseling psychology, we use the term *victim mentality*. Sure, there are millions of individuals who have suffered incomprehensible abuses throughout their lives. Some people *really have* been victims. These are not the individuals I am referring to.

What I would like you to consider is how you may be *acting* like a victim in your own life. These types of attitudes are referred to as taking a *victim stance* or having a *victim mentality*. A person who takes a *victim stance* avoids doing what they need (or want) to do in a variety of ways, without even being aware of how they are self-sabotaging.

The following examples are referred to as *thinking errors* or *cognitive distortions*, principals developed by Dr. Aaron Beck:

Blaming: "It is your fault that I was late for the job interview. You are never on time!"

Excuse making: "I am just too old to return to college!"

Rationalizing: "If you had a hard life like me, you would drink, too!"

Self-pity: "I do not have any good friends…people just do not like me."

Polarized thinking: "If I cannot do it perfectly, why even try!"

Do you see the patterns with this type of thinking? Thinking from the *victim stance* does not allow you to change. Thinking in these unhealthy ways makes you a prisoner of your own mind. Instead of playing the victim of circumstances, do something differently. Start taking accountability for the part you play in the dysfunctional areas of your life. Instead of blaming someone for making you late, ask yourself how you can be prompt next time. Instead of telling yourself *I am just too old*, tell yourself I am *not* too old, and I could do _____ if I really wanted to. Get in the habit of using "I

WILL" and "I CAN" statements. Thinking and speaking in this manner puts you back in control of the areas in your life you can change. For example:

I do not like being poor, so *I will* begin looking for a better paying job.

I will begin to increase my circle of friends by joining a club or taking a class.

Even if I cannot do something perfectly, *I can* do my best! That is good enough.

My life has been hard, but drinking over it is my choice. *I can* quit if I want to.

Using these four little words – I CAN and I WILL - takes you from being a victim to being the catalyst for change in your life. Do you not like where you are at in life? Do something about it. Take the advice of Woody Allen, who said "Eighty percent of success is showing up." All you must do is begin, so what are you waiting for? STOP BEING A VICTIM.

Day 23

"Nobody can make you feel inferior without your permission." – Eleanor Roosevelt

Are you influenced by what other people think or say about you? I think that we all are to some degree. The honest truth is that *what others think about you is none of your business*. When we base our self-concept on what other people think and say about us, we essentially give them power over our lives. We let other people define who we are and who we are not. We let others tell us what we can and cannot do and what we can and cannot be. THIS TYPE OF THINKING IS WRONG, highly unproductive and self-defeating. What other people think and say about you is only their *opinion* and theirs alone. When we hear negative messages all of our lives, as many of us have, we begin to *believe* in the negative messages and the negative messages become our *reality*.

What makes something true? Have you ever given this any thought? Take, for example, a group of first graders. Think of one of these first graders who is exceptionally gifted – a really smart boy with an unusually high I.Q. who reads and writes far beyond the first grade level. This boy is popular among his peers as well. Now think of the first grader who lacks motivation, lacks self-esteem and might be considered the outsider among his peers. He struggles with his homework, with making friends and generally dislikes school.

Let us assume that the *very gifted* first grader is told by his parents, his teachers and his peers that he is stupid. Stupid, stupid, stupid. This poor little boy is told that he will probably be held back a year, will have to attend tutoring just to catch up and will probably always struggle in school. *Remember*, if we are told something enough times and we do not challenge whether what is said to us is *true*, we begin to believe what other people tell us IS THE TRUTH, even though it is not. IT IS JUST THEIR OPINION OF US, NOTHING ELSE.

Next take the first grader who struggles in school. This is the outsider, the unpopular and insecure little boy. If this little first grader is constantly told by his parents, teachers and peers that he is smart, gifted and quite popular, guess what happens? The little boy begins to believe it. He begins to excel at his school work, he begins to make friends and he begins to love school. The difference between the two first graders is that the first believed in all of the *lies* he was told. He *accepted* the *negative* feedback he received from his parents, teachers and peers. The negative feedback became his TRUTH. The second first grader also believed in what others told him, but the difference was that the feedback he received was *positive*. He began to believe he was smart, gifted and popular. The positive messages became his TRUTH.

Most damage is done to the human psyche during our childhood years, when our little minds are uncorrupted, blank canvases. Damage done in our formative years can be difficult to correct, but it *can* be corrected. If you are reading this, you already have the capacity to change your mind about what you *do* and *do not* believe about yourself. Firstly, remember that WHAT OTHERS THINK ABOUT YOU IS NONE OF YOUR BUSINESS. Secondly, remember that when we put too much stock into what others say about us, WE GIVE THEM POWER OVER OUR LIVES.

Begin today to re-write the script of your life. Do not believe what other people say about you. ONLY YOU CAN BE THE JUDGE OF WHO YOU ARE AND WHO YOU ARE BECOMING. Start today to challenge what you believe about yourself. All you must do is begin.

Day 24

"Sought through prayer and meditation to improve our conscious contact with God, as we understood Him, praying only for knowledge of His will for us and the power to carry that out." – Step 11 of Alcoholics Anonymous

In today's lightning-fast paced world, people are constantly trying to stay ahead of the pack. If you are anything like me, your alarm clock seems to go off earlier and earlier in order to squeeze in just as much as you can on any given day. We spend countless hours at work trying to impress our bosses with the hope of a positive appraisal. We run out the door each morning, eating our breakfast from a greasy fast-food joint and drink copious amounts of caffeinated beverages just to stay awake to do more. *More, more, more.* We neglect eating lunch some days, with the belief that we are simply too busy.

We are more connected with our peers and associates than ever – email, text messaging and social networking are literally just the press of a button or a swipe away. We pay our bills online, order food online and spend untold amounts of money - mostly money that we do not even have to spend - trying to look our best.

It seems there are not enough hours in the day and the technology industry seems to have caught on to this trend. We are *busier* than ever but things are *more convenient* than ever. I think it is fair to say that we worship progress, success and keeping up with the Jones' more than anything else. Is it not easier than ever to stay connected to our work, to our friends and family, to the news and to our finances than ever before? If your answer is "Yes, of course it is easy to stay connected! I have a smart phone that does everything!" I then ask you this: Just what do you worship?

The eleventh step of a 12-step recovery program asks us to seek through the practices of prayer and meditation an improved contact with *the One who created us* – as we understand Him. This step asks us to pray *only* for knowledge of His will for us and the power to carry that out. That it is. I think that this powerful step applies to *all* people, recovering or not. Ask yourself this: when was the last time you prayed? When was the last time you sat alone – in complete silence - and just listened for God's will for your life? When is the last time you said the simplest of all prayers: *Thank you, God.* If you struggle with the concept of God or a Higher Power, that is okay. You can begin by meditating on anything that brings you into the moment. Do you like nature? The beach? Do you have a love for art or music? Pick something that is pure, good and brings you joy. Find twenty minutes each morning - or whenever you can - and meditate on the thing or topic of your choosing. Mornings are probably best, before the chaos of the day sets in.

Always do the things that are most important to you upon awakening. *Meditation, simply put, means focusing your mind – 100% of your mind – on some area. It is that simple.* Meditation promotes relaxation, a renewal of energy, peace and a feeling of connectedness with something greater than you. Just as you would click a button on your smartphone to "connect" with a friend, you can "connect" with something more powerful than you by meditating on this thing. **You worship what you spend the most time on.** Do you spend most of your time making money? Then you certainly worship money. Do you spend most of your time watching T.V.? Then you certainly worship T.V. How about the battery of social networking options we have these days? Do you spend most of your free time surfing the internet? Then you certainly worship the internet Gods.

SLOW DOWN and work on your INNER SELF. Work on your relationship with something more powerful than you. I choose God, but you can choose whatever you would like. All you must do is begin.

Day 25

"Aim at nothing and you will succeed." –
Anonymous

Are you a finisher? Just how many projects do you
have going at any given time? Are you repainting
the bathroom, building a play set for your children
and organizing your closet all at the same time?
Just how many projects have you actually
completed? If you are anything like me, you
probably take on *way* to much in life. *Are you like*
an arrow without a target? We waste lots of time
trying to do too much. What if you put everything
else on hold - just for today - and focused your
energy on completing *one task* and *stayed* on that
task until it was finished?

When I purchased my first home some time ago, I
got an "as-is" deal on a small home on some
wooded land too good to pass up. Upon seeing the
home for the first time, I was warned that this was
a true fixer-upper. *Great!* I thought. *I have all the*
skills to do whatever I need to do to this place and
I am getting a great deal. I can just work on one
room at a time and have this place looking sharp
in a year or so. Boy was I wrong. I greatly
underestimated my ability to begin a job and *finish*
it until the end.

Once I signed the paperwork to my new home, I
began making a list of what needed to be done:
new tile flooring throughout, tearing down and

putting up a few walls, rewiring and insulating the pole barn, replacing the kitchen counter, putting in new cupboards, redoing the drywall in the spare bedrooms and replacing the bathtub…just to name a few. By the time I had finished my list, I literally had over one hundred improvements I *needed* or *wanted* to make. Do you think I started slowly, as I had planned and worked on one task at a time?

In the excitement of being a new home owner, I took on too many projects at once and never seemed to finish any of them. I started tearing out all the old carpeting and replacing the sub-floor, one sheet of wood at a time. I was hanging drywall in the big pole barn out back, doing some landscaping, upgrading the wiring and putting in new cupboards – all at the same time. For the first year I literally lived in a construction zone. I did not seem to be getting anything done. I got frustrated and I started making mistakes. My mistakes made me more frustrated. It was not until a dear old friend of mine came to visit that I had my "ah-ha" moment.

My friend Jerry walked in my back door and shouted "Pauly, what happened in here? Do you have a whole crew working for you or what?" *Nope, just me, Jerry*. Jerry had made his living as a carpenter for the past twenty-five years and gave me a piece of advice that sticks with me today. He said "Buddy, this ain't a race. Slow down. Just like you are learning to live *one day at a time*, only take on *one project at a time*. Do something once and be done with it. Do you have time to do all these projects over if you don't do them right the first time? I doubt it!"

Here is my suggestion for you: DO ONE THING AT A TIME AND DO IT WELL. BE THE ARROW WITH A TARGET. Slow down and enjoy the work, whatever it might be. All you must do is begin - but finish what you start!

Day 26

"Finish each day and be done with it." – Ralph Waldo Emerson

There is so much truth in the simplicity of this concept. Finish each day and be done with it. There is no use in carrying the problems of today into tomorrow. What can you do about the past? Nothing, but most people spend plenty of time worrying about or regretting the things they did not do *yesterday*. We worry that we wasted our time, said something we should not have, or missed an opportunity. Yesterday is gone. Take it out with the trash. Stop carrying yesterday around with you.

Every Tuesday evening I roll our garbage can out to the road. The mighty can holds all the trash from the past week and most weeks it gets quite full. We try to not waste anything, but some weeks we will throw away our leftovers, old tattered clothing, shredded paperwork and so on. Pretty typical garbage for most people. I promise that you will *never* find me sifting through our garbage once it has been taken to the road. Once something hits the garbage can, I have come to the conclusion that it is *garbage*. I let the garbage company do their job. They pick up our garbage and haul it away to the landfill. I can also promise that you will *never* find me at the land fill, looking for our discarded items, wondering *should I have thrown away that old sweater? I wonder if that half-eaten pizza is out here somewhere…I wish I would not have thrown that away. I wish I would have saved that freezer burned ice cream, that milk that had gone bad, all those old magazines and all those grass clippings.* NO WAY! Once I take out my garbage it is gone forever. I will never see it again because it is of no use to me or anyone else.

Start today off the way God intended you to. Leave the troubles, worries and misfortunes of yesterday where they belong. In Isaiah 43:18-19, it reads *"Remember not the former things, nor consider the things of old. Behold, I am doing a new thing; now it springs forth, do you not perceive it? I will make a way in the wilderness and rivers in the desert."* Be grateful that God has given you yet another opportunity to live another day. A fresh new start is a privilege and it is the most precious thing we have been promised. Start today off with an attitude of gratitude and do your best to keep your mind where your feet are - IN TODAY.

Put all your worries, all your mistakes and all your regrets from yesterday in the garbage can and leave them there. Don't go sifting through all your old garbage. Leave it alone. Just begin.

Day 27

"Do not walk where the path may lead, go instead where there is no path and leave a trail." –
Oscar Wilde

The media bombards us with images of who we are supposed to be, what we should look like, what kinds of clothes we should wear and who our friends should be. We are constantly told what career path we should take, where we should live, where we should invest our money and how we should plan, plan, plan for an *unknown* and *scary* future. It is all too easy to get caught up in the popularity tornado. We begin to lose parts of ourselves by being who we think we *ought* to be and not being who we *really* are. We seem to be living under an attitude of conformity. A good paying job, a nice car, well-adjusted kids, the right clothes and popular social circles seem to top the list for the criteria of *fitting in*.

The biggest problem with fitting in is that it is *boring* and it is *safe*. What fun is it to do what everyone else is doing? Not much, if you ask me. It really says a lot about a person who forgets who they are in order to become who others want them to be. I have seen this all too often in my work as an addiction treatment professional. People become disillusioned and chameleon like. They try to fit in with everyone, try to please everybody and yearn for acceptance and approval. All they are doing is attempting to fill a God-sized hole. The result is never good, as most people find that it is impossible to be *everything* to *everybody*.

One of my favorite custom motorcycle builders used to make some of the most beautiful, mechanically perfect machines on the road. At around 50,000 dollars a pop, these hand-built, custom bikes were a little out of my price range. However, I always admired the builder – he hand crafted each frame, built many of his own parts from raw hunks of steel and tuned each motor using nothing but his own ear. His paint work was completely flawless. The smallest of details were considered, right down to the spokes on the wheels. They were absolutely gorgeous machines made in the good old U.S.A. I have heard that each bike took anywhere from four to six months - start to finish - until it was completed. Old-world, highly skilled builders like this are becoming less and less commonplace, as most builders opt to go for quantity instead of quality. This is a shame, because we are losing some very talented craftsmen along the way.

Several years ago this particular builder must have gotten a deal he could not refuse. He stopped building custom bikes and sold his name and brand to a production company overseas. His once hand-crafted, one-of-a-kind motorcycles, parts and accessories are now being mass produced in China. Every bike that rolls off the assembly line looks like the one before it. There is zero originality, zero quality and zero soul in these once awesome creations which used to be forged from steel, sweat and blood. This particular builder sold out for fame and prestige. He did what everyone else was doing. He did the popular thing and chased the almighty dollar, losing himself along the way. His company is now but a dream. He no longer builds motorcycles and no one seems to know what has happened to him. The once creative and innovate soul who refused to conform to industry standards is now all but forgotten.

DO NOT LET THIS BE YOU. I am guessing that you are not a famous custom motorcycle builder and likely have no desire to be one. This lesson *does* apply to you, however. Are you *selling out* just to fit it? Are you going against your own morals, values and beliefs just to gain some level of acceptance? Do you regularly say what you truly believe, or do you sit quietly in the back row of life and agree with what everyone else is saying? Have you lost your voice? If so, it is not too late. Just be you. Do what you want to do, even if it is not the popular thing. Say what you need to say. Do not worry about being judged. Who cares if you fit in? Do not listen to the opinions of others and certainly do not follow trends.

Begin today to stand up for yourself. Fight for what you believe is true and important in your *own* life. Do not let others tell you who you are supposed to be. They do not know. All you must do is begin, TODAY, to live the kind of life that makes you happy. As author Jason Mason once said, "You were born an original…do *not* die a copy!"

Day 28

"Rich people have small T.V.s and big libraries, and poor people have small libraries and big T.V.s" – Zig Ziglar

I am not entirely sure what the famous motivational speaker Zig Ziglar meant when he said this, but when I recite it to myself I can think about this statement in several ways. The quotation might suggest that rich people might be more educated than poor people. This is sometimes true, I suppose. Mr. Ziglar might also be speaking about the accumulation of knowledge as the path towards financial well-being. Again, this is might be true in some cases. It is true that reading and studying can yield an education. It is also true than an education can lead to a better paying job and more financial security.

However, the *primary* meanings I take from Mr. Ziglar's words are this:

People that are *rich* are rich in faith, spirit and knowledge.

People that are *poor* are poor in faith, spirit and knowledge.

Being rich does not necessarily mean *financially rich* and being poor does not necessarily mean *financially poor*.

The Holy Bible speaks many times about being *rich in spiritual, heavenly things,* not *material things.* This is just one example, from Matthew 6:19-21 *"Do not lay up for yourselves treasures on earth, where moths and rust destroy and where thieves break in and steal, but lay up for yourselves treasures in heaven, where neither moth nor rust destroys and where thieves do not break in and steal. For where your treasure is, there your heart will be also."*

I like to think that Mr. Ziglar was referring to a spiritual library. This is something we all should have if we are truly on the path to a better, more fulfilling life. A *spiritual library* could simply consist of a Bible, a motivational book, a recovery oriented book, a self-improvement book, or a book of prayers. Remember what makes you what you are? Remember what defines who you are as a person and who you are becoming? If you forgot, here it is once more: *You can tell what is important to a person by how they spend their time and by what they make a priority in their lives.* You can *say* that God, faith and working to become a better person are your primary focuses in life. If you spend all of your time watching your flat-screen T.V., carelessly spending your money, hoarding your possessions and generally living a life void of faith, God and study, these things are obviously not as important as you claim they are.

While I do enjoy watching T.V. on occasion, I find that I get the most fulfillment from studying spiritual things, meditating and praying and trying to learn God's will for me. Try it today. Turn off the T.V. and turn on your mind to the possibilities that await you through the study of spiritual things. As always, all you must do is begin.

Day 29

"The road to success is dotted with many tempting parking spaces." – Will Rogers

Did you know that the famous author Stephen King had his book *Carrie* rejected some *thirty times* before he found a publisher? Did you know that probably one of the best known sports figures of our time, Michael Jordan, was actually *cut* from his high school basketball team? Take for instance Walt Disney. Did you know that when he attempted to sell MGM studios his idea of Mickey Mouse in 1920's, he was told that his idea was no good and would never work? What do all these highly successful individuals have in common, you ask? *They never said never and they never gave up.* Even when it looked like their dreams would fizzle away, when people told them *no* - again and again - they kept their eyes fixed forward and kept trying.

Sure, it would have been all too easy for Stephen King, Michael Jordan or Walt Disney to find a parking spot along the road to success and say "Well, at least I tried…it was not meant to be." Look at what these individuals have achieved in their lives. Their successes did not come overnight and certainly did not come easy. They chopped wood and carried water for as long as it took to realize their dreams *until their dreams became reality*. Think about your own life. You do not need to become a famous author, athlete, or entrepreneur. All you need is a goal and the passion to never give up on that goal. As Thomas Jefferson said, *"Nothing can stop the man with the right mental attitude from achieving his goal; nothing on earth can help the man with the wrong mental attitude."*

Are you looking for instant gratification? If you are, look on. Achieving your goals and dreams will require discipline, determination and plenty of hard work. Remember, all you must do is begin and *continue* beginning each new day.

Day 30

"Everything can be taken from a man but one thing - the last of human freedoms is the ability to choose one's attitude in any given set of circumstances, to choose one's own way."
Viktor E. Frankl -

If you do not know who Viktor Frankl is, I assure you that reading about his life and legacy will be an endeavor well worth your while. Frankl was an Austrian psychiatrist and neurologist. He was also a Holocaust survivor. He has written several books detailing his experiences in Nazi concentration camps, all of which are incredibly inspirational. He found that no matter what the Nazi soldiers took from him, no matter what they did to him, they could not take away his choice in attitude. He found that maintaining a positive attitude of hope was the *only* thing he could control - and control it he did.

For the past twenty-nine days you have read passages about changing your thinking and your behaviors. You have learned about the power in setting and achieving goals, having faith and following God's will no matter what. You have also learned to accept the things in life you cannot change. You have learned about the importance of action steps and not making excuses; about the dangers of procrastination and other self-defeating behaviors. You have learned some fancy psychological terms and have also learned to cut out unhealthy things in your life. The one thing I would like you to think about for the rest of the day is your ATTITUDE. Choosing the right mental attitude is a something you must do every day if you wish to create peace and happiness.

As it is written on the pages of the Twelve Steps and Twelve Traditions of Alcoholics Anonymous, we have the choice to employ NEW ATTITUDES whenever we choose to. Just for today, choose a NEW ATTITUDE. Make it one of gratitude, hope and excitement for life. You can choose to live life on the sidelines, or choose to live your life on the field.

I choose to live my life on the field. It is a much better view and there is much more action. Sure, I get knocked down, bruised and banged up from time to time, but that is what *living* is all about. As the saying goes from one of my favorite movies, *The Shawshank Redemption* - GET BUSY LIVING OR GET BUSY DYING. The choice is yours. Life is what you make of it. *Begin today to live your life like you really mean it.*

Get busy chopping wood and carrying water. Remember: the good life is not free and it is certainly not easy, but it is all worth all the hard work it in the end.

ABOUT THE AUTHOR

Paul J. Wolanin has been working as an Addiction Treatment professional for the past nine years, with a background in psychology and addictive disorders. He holds a Bachelor's degree in Psychology and Addictive Disorders from Central Michigan University and a Master's Degree in Psychology from the Chicago School of Professional Psychology. He is also a Certified Alcohol and Drug Counselor. Paul is passionate about giving to others what was once given to him - another chance at life and the knowledge that anything is possible for he who believes.
He currently works as an addictions therapist at a residential center in Michigan, where he is part of a multidisciplinary team who treats individuals with addictive and mental health disorders.

You can follow Paul's blog at:
http://freedomthroughchange76.blogspot.com/

Visit his official website:
http://freedomthroughchange.com/

Visit him on Facebook:
https://www.facebook.com/ChoppingWood76

On Twitter:
https://twitter.com/Choppingwood76

IMPORTANT: Please turn the page! ☺

Review Request

If you have enjoyed this book I would be very grateful if you would post a positive review. Your support means a lot to me and it really does make a difference in the further direction of my writing. I am always open to suggestions and I am always listening to my readers!

If you would like to leave me a review, it's easy! All you have to do is go to the review section of this book's **Amazon.com** page and click on the big shiny button that says "Write a customer review."

Thank you again for your support.

Yours in recovery,

Paul

Keep Your Axes Sharp.

Keep Chopping Wood

And

Carrying Water.

CPSIA information can be obtained at www.ICGtesting.com
Printed in the USA
BVOW07s0055070714

358161BV00006B/271/P

9 781493 710898